ALTERNATOR
BOOKS™

BREAKTHROUGHS IN THE SEARCH FOR EXTRATERRESTRIAL LIFE

Karen Latchana Kenney

Lerner Publications ◆ Minneapolis

Lerner Publications Company
A division of Lerner Publishing Group, Inc.
241 First Avenue North
Minneapolis, MN 55401 USA

For reading levels and more information, look up this title at www.lernerbooks.com.

Main body text set in Aptifer Sans LT Pro Regular 12/18.
Typeface provided by Linotype AG.

Library of Congress Cataloging-in-Publication Data

Names: Kenney, Karen Latchana, author.
Title: Breakthroughs in the search for extraterrestrial life / Karen Latchana Kenney.
Description: Minneapolis : Lerner Publications, [2019] | Series: Space exploration.
    Alternator Books | Audience: Ages 8–12. | Audience: Grades 4 to 6. | Includes
    bibliographical references and index.
Identifiers: LCCN 2018016811 (print) | LCCN 2018034691 (ebook) |
    ISBN 9781541543768 (eb pdf) | ISBN 9781541538726 (lb : alk. paper)
Subjects: LCSH: Search for Extraterrestrial Intelligence (Study group : U.S.)—
    Juvenile literature. | Life on other planets—Juvenile literature. | Interstellar
    communication—Juvenile literature. | Outer space—Exploration—Juvenile
    literature.
Classification: LCC QB54 (ebook) | LCC QB54 .K46 2019 (print) | DDC 576.8/39—dc23

LC record available at https://lccn.loc.gov/2018016811

Manufactured in the United States of America
1-45055-35882-7/23/2018

Contents

A LIFE-FRIENDLY PLANET?

This image shows star trails, or the motion of stars in the sky, over the High Accuracy Radial velocity Planet Searcher in Chile.

In July 2005, European astronomers began watching a star 11 **light-years** away from Earth called Ross 128. The astronomers used the High Accuracy Radial velocity Planet Searcher (HARPS). The scientific instrument was made to search for **exoplanets**—planets orbiting stars outside of our solar system.

Ross 128 is a red dwarf star. This
is one of the most common types of
stars in the universe. Red dwarfs
are smaller and cooler than our sun.

An artist's image shows the planet Ross 128b with the star Ross 128 in the background.

Twelve years later, in November 2017, the astronomers announced that they found a planet similar in size to Earth near the star. The astronomers called the planet Ross 128b. It seemed rocky, and possibly in its star's **Goldilocks zone**— not too close or too far away from the star. This meant its temperatures could be similar to Earth's, and it was possible for water to exist there. These conditions are ideal for life to exist on Earth. Scientists wonder if **extraterrestrial** life exists on Ross 128b.

An illustration of Ross 128b imagines what the surface of the planet might look like, including rocky features and water.

THE SEARCH FOR LIFE

This illustration shows Kenneth Arnold flying by Mount Rainier in the United States, where he says he saw bright flashes in the sky from several flying objects.

For many years, people have wondered if life exists on other planets. Do aliens have spaceships and visit us here on Earth? Many people have reported seeing **unidentified flying objects (UFOs)** in the sky. One of the first UFO stories came from pilot Kenneth Arnold in 1947. He saw nine circular

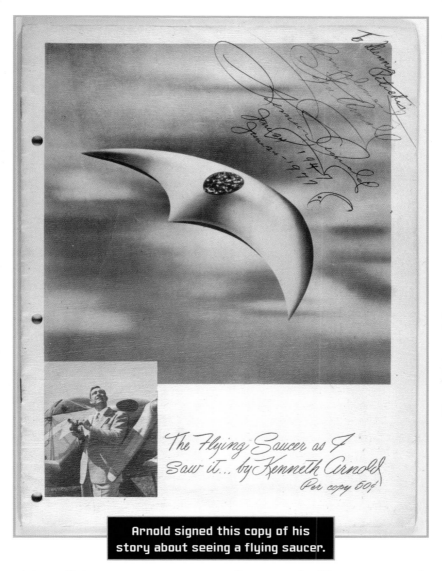

objects flying as a group at superfast speeds. His story spread across the United States, and soon more UFO sightings made newspaper headlines. Some people have taken photos and videos of strange objects in the sky. But no one proved that UFOs exist.

An artist's image shows *Pioneer 10* flying toward Neptune.

FIRST PIONEERS

In the 1950s, humans began sending out our own kind of UFOs—the first space probes—to explore our solar system. In 1972 and 1973, NASA sent *Pioneer 10* and *Pioneer 11* to fly by Jupiter and Saturn. The probes carried messages in case they found intelligent alien life. The messages showed a drawing of a man and a woman, a diagram of our solar system, and the position of our sun in space. The diagram was a map to help alien life find us on Earth.

Two probes sent in 1977 had an even more detailed message for aliens. The *Voyager 1* and *Voyager 2* probes each carried a golden disk. On the disks were images, music, sounds, and greetings in different languages from people on Earth. NASA lost contact with the *Pioneer* probes in 1995 and 2003 but is still tracking the *Voyager* probes. They continue traveling through space.

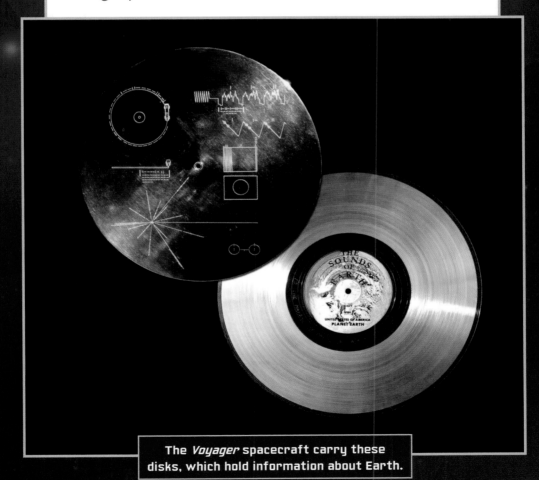

The *Voyager* spacecraft carry these disks, which hold information about Earth.

SEARCHING OUR SOLAR SYSTEM

Scientists are very interested in the surface of Mars. They study the rocks and soil searching for elements that may be signs the planet once hosted life.

Scientists begin searching for life by looking for its ingredients. They think life on Earth formed from six chemical elements: carbon, hydrogen, nitrogen, oxygen, phosphorus, and sulfur. Life also needs water, energy, nutrients, and protection from harmful energy in space.

If a planet or moon has some of these ingredients, life may exist in some form there. One of the most interesting planets in the search for life is Mars. It has evidence of water—lots of water. Oceans and rivers may have once flowed across the surface of Mars. And frozen water may be just below the planet's surface.

An artist's image shows what Mars may have looked like billions of years ago, with an ocean covering much of the planet.

STEM FOCUS

Scientists are still discovering new forms of life on Earth. Some creatures called **extremophiles** live in extreme environments such as dry deserts. Some even live by hot vents deep in the ocean. They use chemicals in the vents as food. Scientists wonder if the oceans on icy moons have hot vents. If they do, life may be swimming under the moons' icy crusts.

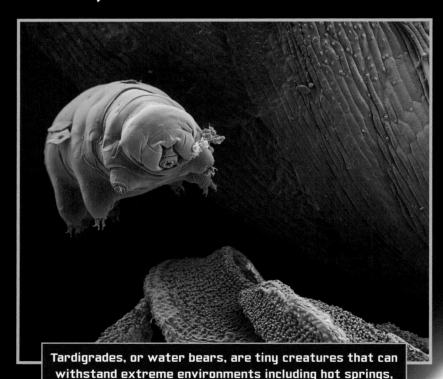

Tardigrades, or water bears, are tiny creatures that can withstand extreme environments including hot springs, deep water, and high levels of dangerous energy.

MARS MISSIONS

Scientists have sent many missions to Mars to search for water and life. One of these missions is the Mars Science Laboratory mission. It put a robotic science laboratory called the *Curiosity* rover on the surface of Mars in 2012. In 2013 *Curiosity* drilled into rocks on Mars. It found carbon, hydrogen, oxygen, sulfur, nitrogen, and phosphorus in the rocks. The rover didn't find life, but these elements were evidence that Mars could have once supported life. The rover also detected methane gas. **Microbes** on Earth release this kind of gas. Could Mars have microbes too?

The *Curiosity* rover took this image of itself on a Martian mountain called Mount Sharp.

Two new missions will land on Mars in the 2020s to continue the search for life. One mission is the *ExoMars* rover. The rover will land in an area scientists believe is likely to hold evidence of life. It will use its state-of-the-art scientific instruments to drill into rocks and soil and analyze them. The *Mars 2020* rover will also search for evidence that microbes once lived on the planet. It will look for signs of what Mars's environment was like in the past to see if it could have once supported life.

ICY MOONS

Astronomers have identified some moons as places to search for life as well. Several moons orbiting Saturn and Jupiter are especially interesting. One is Europa, which orbits Jupiter. The moon has an icy crust that may cover a vast ocean. NASA plans to visit the moon in the 2020s with its *Europa Clipper* spacecraft. It will fly by the moon and study it using cameras and scientific instruments. The Hubble Space Telescope detected evidence of water plumes coming from the moon in 2012. If they still exist when *Europa Clipper* arrives, the spacecraft will fly through them to find out what they are made of.

The *Cassini* spacecraft saw similar plumes coming from Enceladus, one of Saturn's moons. *Cassini* discovered hydrogen in the plumes. NASA may send a mission there soon to find out more.

This image shows the surface of Europa. The water plumes are around the bottom of the moon.

READY TO RECEIVE

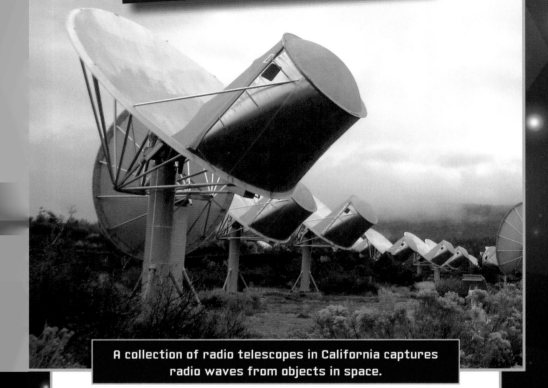

A collection of radio telescopes in California captures radio waves from objects in space.

One way astronomers search for life in space is through **radio waves**. We can listen to music sent out by radio stations on Earth through radio waves. Radio waves also travel toward Earth from objects in space such as planets, stars, and comets. Detecting radio waves from space takes high-powered technology.

STARTING SETI

In 1984 the Search for Extraterrestrial Intelligence (SETI) Institute formed. SETI searches for signals from space using different telescopes, including the Allen Telescope Array in California. This array consists of forty-two radio telescopes that work together to collect data by observing our sky and areas at the center of our galaxy.

SETI looks for signals of a certain frequency, one that natural objects probably can't make. These signals could be a message from extraterrestrial life, but SETI hasn't yet received such a confirmed signal. Scientists working on an early version of SETI did pick up an unusual signal of unknown origin in 1977. The signal lasted for seventy-two seconds, but it never repeated.

Part of the Allen Telescope Array in Hat Creek, California

A software engineer at SETI reviews data collected by the Allen Telescope Array.

SETI is also watching for visual signals from space in the form of laser **beacons**. The institute's researchers use powerful reflecting telescopes to observe light in the night sky. These telescopes use a large mirror to gather and focus light. SETI has a light-measuring instrument on the Nickel Telescope at the Lick Observatory in California. It can detect flashes of light, such as the light that could come from a laser beacon many light-years away from Earth.

BREAKTHROUGH INITIATIVES

A few other research programs are scanning the skies for messages from intelligent life. One big program is Breakthrough Initiatives. Its Breakthrough Listen project uses three large telescopes to detect signals. The Robert C. Byrd Green Bank Telescope has a 328-foot-wide (100 m) dish. Scientists use it, along with the Parkes Telescope, a very sensitive telescope in Australia, to scan the stars closest to Earth. They use the Automated Planet Finder Telescope at the Lick Observatory to search for laser beacons. The powerful telescope could spot a light equal to that of a typical light bulb shining from 25 trillion miles (40 trillion km) away.

The Robert C. Byrd Green Bank Telescope in West Virginia is able to detect very weak radio signals from space.

EXPLORING THE STARS

Michel Mayor (*left*) and Didier Queloz stand in front of telescopes in Chile they used to search for exoplanets.

Humans didn't know until the 1990s if planets outside our solar system existed. In 1995 astronomers Michel Mayor and Didier Queloz found the first exoplanet orbiting a sunlike star. It was one of the first of many exoplanet discoveries. Scientists have since found more than thirty-seven hundred exoplanets, and that number rises daily. Astronomers think at least one exoplanet orbits every star in space.

One big planet hunter is the Kepler Space Telescope. It has revealed more than twenty-three hundred exoplanets. Some are especially interesting in the search for life. They are in the Goldilocks zones of their solar systems. Like on Ross 128b, temperatures on these planets may be just right for life to exist.

ALIEN ATMOSPHERES

Large telescopes can detect what is in the atmospheres of exoplanets. When a planet moves between Earth and its star, we can see the light from the star as it shines through the planet's atmosphere. Different gases affect light differently as it passes through. By looking at these differences in the light, astronomers can figure out which gases are present. A planet's **biosignature** shows gases in its atmosphere possibly produced by life. Oxygen and methane gas are two that could be signs of life. Oxygen could mean plants and bacteria are on a planet. Methane could mean microbes live there.

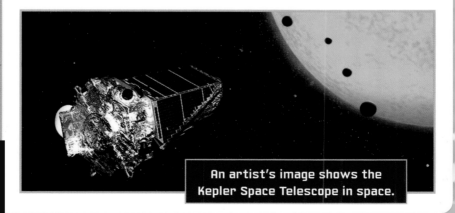

An artist's image shows the Kepler Space Telescope in space.

Scientists have seen some distant atmospheres with the Hubble Space Telescope. But they will soon get a much clearer picture of these atmospheres. The James Webb Space Telescope will look at the atmospheres of rocky planets similar to Earth in size and in the Goldilocks zones of their solar systems. This powerful telescope will launch in 2020. Astronomers hope to find an exoplanet with a biosignature similar to Earth's.

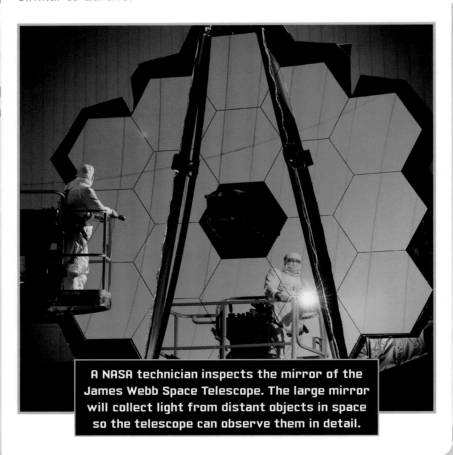

A NASA technician inspects the mirror of the James Webb Space Telescope. The large mirror will collect light from distant objects in space so the telescope can observe them in detail.

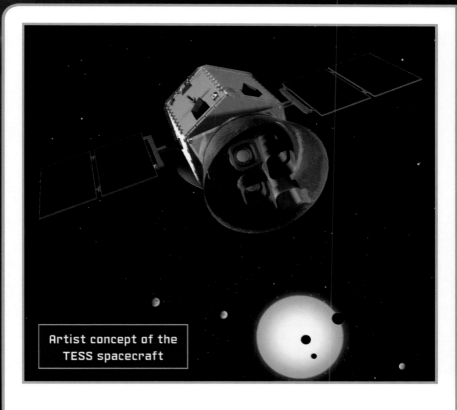

Artist concept of the
TESS spacecraft

FINDING SMALL EXOPLANETS

Another instrument, the Transiting Exoplanet Survey Satellite (TESS), launched in April 2018. In a two-year mission, it will survey two hundred thousand stars to look for planets around them. The James Webb Space Telescope will study some of these planets in depth. And scientists are building the two largest telescopes ever made on Earth. The Extremely Large Telescope and the Giant Magellan Telescope will start operating in Chile in the 2020s. They will look for small, rocky exoplanets—the kind that might support life.

STEM FOCUS

The Extremely Large Telescope will be the world's largest telescope. Its main mirror will be 128 feet (39 m) wide. This mirror is made of 798 segments that fit together like a puzzle. Technicians make each segment precisely. First, they heat liquid glass to 2,552°F (1,400°C). They pour the liquid into a mold and let it cool for weeks. Then machines polish the mirror until it is smooth. Any errors might stop the telescope from forming clear images.

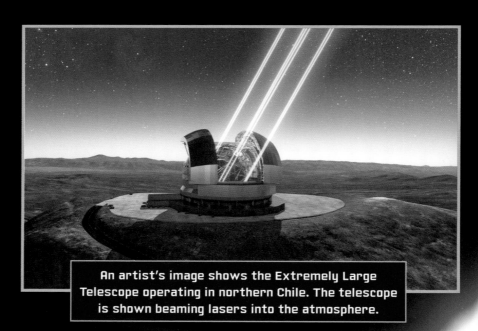

An artist's image shows the Extremely Large Telescope operating in northern Chile. The telescope is shown beaming lasers into the atmosphere.

The search for extraterrestrial life is gaining speed as we find more and more exoplanets. What discoveries will the 2020s bring? New telescopes may just find the first evidence of life on other planets.

The TESS spacecraft will look for thousands of exoplanets orbiting around some of the brightest stars in the sky.

A distant planet orbits a star called HD 209458. The star is 150 light-years from Earth.

WHAT THE TECH?

The James Webb Space Telescope is an infrared telescope. It will detect distant infrared waves, energy that people cannot see with their eyes. To find this faint energy made by heat, the telescope needs to be very cold. That's why it has a sun shield. This shield will face the moon, Earth, and sun to shade the telescope's cameras and instruments from heat and light. The sun shield will reflect light and heat back out into space. It will keep the telescope at –370°F (–223°C). Meanwhile, the outside of the sun shield will reach 185°F (85°C).

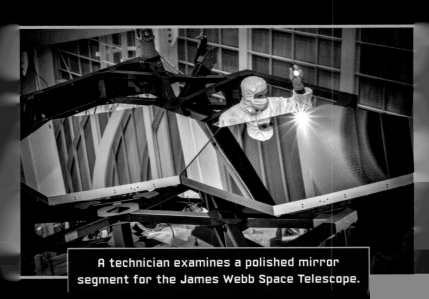

A technician examines a polished mirror segment for the James Webb Space Telescope.

beacons: lights used as signals or warnings

biosignature: substances found in the atmospheres of planets that show life may exist there

exoplanets: planets orbiting stars outside of our solar system

extraterrestrial: coming from or existing outside of Earth

extremophiles: living things that thrive in extreme environments on Earth

Goldilocks zone: the area around a star where the temperature is just right for liquid water to exist on a planet

light-years: units for measuring distance in space, which is the distance light can travel in one year

microbes: very tiny living things that can be seen only through a microscope

radio waves: one type of energy wave in the electromagnetic spectrum, which also includes the light we can see

unidentified flying objects (UFOs): mysterious, unexplainable objects seen in the sky

FURTHER INFORMATION

Aguilar, David A. *Alien Worlds: Your Guide to Extraterrestrial Life.* Washington, DC: National Geographic, 2013.

ESA Kids: Are We Alone?
https://www.esa.int/esaKIDSen/SEM3NFXPXPF_LifeinSpace_0.html

Europa: Jupiter's Ocean World
https://spaceplace.nasa.gov/europa/en/

Exoplanets
http://idahoptv.org/sciencetrek/topics/exoplanets/facts.cfm

Kenney, Karen Latchana. *Mysterious UFOs and Aliens.* Minneapolis: Lerner Publications, 2018.

Oachs, Emily Rose. *UFOs.* Minneapolis: Bellwether Media, 2019.

Silverman, Buffy. *Mars Missions: A Space Discovery Guide.* Minneapolis: Lerner Publications, 2017.

What Is an Exoplanet?
https://spaceplace.nasa.gov/all-about-exoplanets/en/

Photo Acknowledgments

Image credits: ESO/A.Santerne (CC BY 4.0), p. 4; ESO/Digitized Sky Survey 2/ Davide De Martin (CC BY 4.0), p. 5; ESO/M. Kornmesser, pp. 6, 13; MARK GARLICK/ SCIENCE PHOTO LIBRARY/Newscom, p. 7; David A. Hardy/Science Source, p. 8; Chronicle/Alamy Stock Photo, p. 9; NASA/Don Davis, p. 10; NASA/JPL-Caltech, pp. 11, 12; Eye of Science/Science Source, p. 14; NASA/JPL-Caltech/MSSS, p. 15; Mike Peel/Wikimedia Commons (CC-BY-SA-4.0), p. 16; NASA, ESA, W. Sparks (STScI), and the USGS Astrogeology Science Center, p. 17; J Brew/Flickr (CC BY-SA 2.0), p. 18; Colby Gutierrez-Kraybill/Wikimedia Commons (CC BY 2.0), p. 19; AP Photo/Marcio Jose Sanchez, p. 20; West Virginia Collection within the Carol M. Highsmith Archive, Library of Congress, Prints and Photographs Division (LC-DIG-highsm-34484), p. 21; Courtesy Geneva Observatory, p. 22; NASA/Chris Gun, p. 24; Courtesy of MIT's Kavli Institute for Astrophysics and Space Research, p. 25; ESO/L. Calçada, p. 26; Orbital ATK/NASA, p. 27; NASA/G. Bacon (STScI/AVL), p. 28; NASA/C. Gunn, p. 29. Design elements: filo/Getty Images; satit sewtiw/Shutterstock.com; Supphachai Salaeman/Shutterstock.com.

Cover: A. Duro/ESO.